# Berets, Beanies, and Booties

## DEBBY WARE

**Martingale**®
& COMPANY

Berets, Beanies, and Booties
© 2007 by Debby Ware

# Martingale®
## & COMPANY

Martingale & Company
20205 144th Ave. NE
Woodinville, WA 98072-8478
www.martingale-pub.com

Projects originally appeared in *Too Cute! Cotton Knits for Toddlers* by Debby Ware, published by Martingale & Company in 2002.

## Credits
CEO & President: Tom Wierzbicki
Publisher: Jane Hamada
Editorial Director: Mary V. Green
Managing Editor: Tina Cook
Technical Editor: Jane Townswick
Copy Editor: Karen Koll
Design Director: Stan Green
Assistant Design Director: Regina Girard
Illustrator: Robin Strobel
Cover & Text Designer: Stan Green
Photographer: Brent Kane

## Mission Statement
Dedicated to providing quality products and service to inspire creativity.

Printed in China
12 11 10 09 08 07          8 7 6 5 4 3 2 1

ISBN: 978-1-56477-830-7

# Contents

# Knitting Basics

There are many different ways to cast on, knit, purl, bind off, decrease, increase, and finish. Use the following techniques for knitting the patterns in this book. For more information on knitting techniques, check your local yarn shop for good knitting reference books, or consider taking classes that will help you widen your repertoire of knitting skills.

## Casting On

The simplest and most common method of casting on is the one-needle cast on.

1.  Make a slipknot and place it on a knitting needle. Put the tail end of the yarn around your left thumb and the other end around your left index finger. Hold both tails together with the other fingers on your left hand.

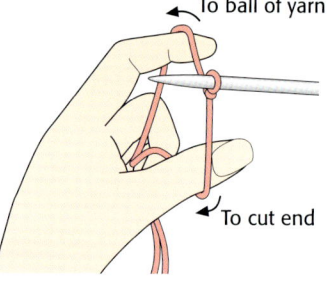

To ball of yarn

To cut end

2.  Insert the needle under the left side of the loop that forms around your left thumb.

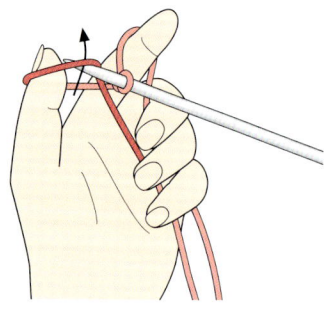

3.  Gradually move the tip of the needle toward the tip of your left index finger. Pick up the yarn around your left index finger and pull it through the loop on your left thumb; then slide the loop off

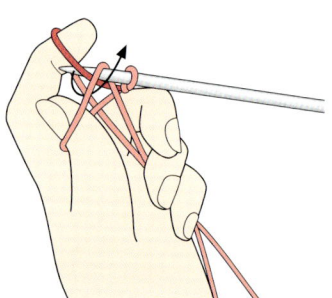

your thumb, completing the cast-on stitch. Pull the yarn gently to snug this stitch around the needle.

4.  Repeat steps 2 and 3 to cast on the desired number of stitches.

## Knitting

1.  To do the knit stitch, hold the yarn in your right hand behind the right needle and insert the right needle from front to back into the stitch on the left needle.

2.  Bring the yarn around the right needle as shown.

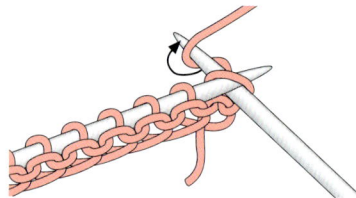

3.  Bring the tip of the right needle through the stitch on the left.

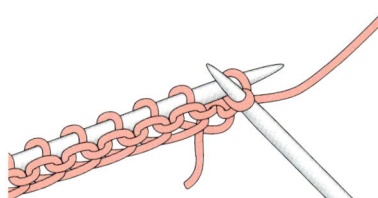

4.  To complete the knit stitch, slip the stitch off the left needle and onto the right one.

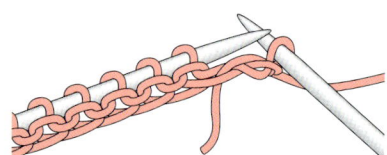

# Purling

1. To do the purl stitch, hold the yarn in your right hand, in front of the right needle.

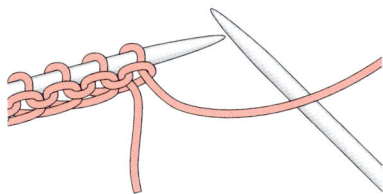

2. Insert the right needle from back to front into the stitch on the left needle, with the right needle in front.

3. Wind the yarn counterclockwise around the right needle.

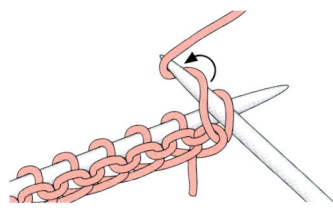

4. Draw the right needle through the stitch from front to back.

5. To complete the purl stitch, slip the stitch off the left needle and onto the right one.

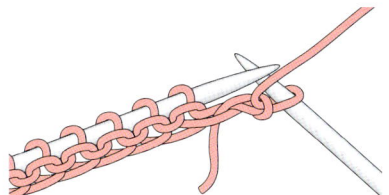

# Increasing

The increases in this book are done by knitting first in the front and then in the back of the same stitch, as shown here. The process is abbreviated as K1f&b in the project instructions.

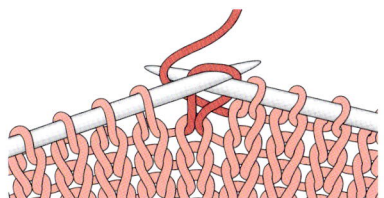

Knit into the front of the next stitch.

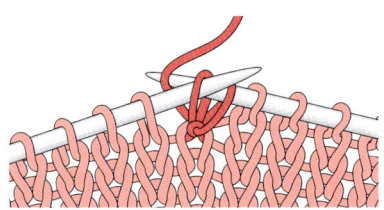

Knit into the back of the same stitch.

# Decreasing

The simplest way to decrease a stitch is to knit two stitches together. The process is abbreviated as K2tog in the project instructions.

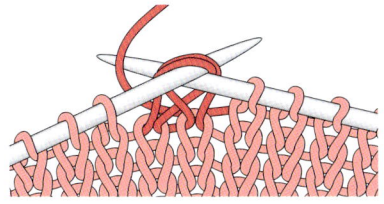

To decrease a stitch on the wrong side of your work, purl 2 stitches together rather than knitting them.

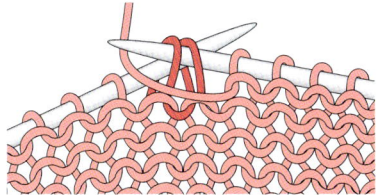

Another method of decreasing is to slip one stitch from the left-hand needle to the right-hand needle without knitting it; then knit the next stitch; then pass the slipped stitch over the just-knitted stitch. This process is abbreviated as sl 1, K 1, psso.

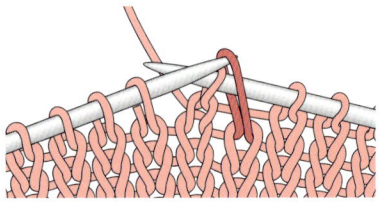

## Binding Off

To bind off stitches, follow these steps.

1.  Knit 2 stitches and pass the first stitch (the one on the right) over the second stitch (the one on the left). Repeat this process to bind off the desired number of stitches.

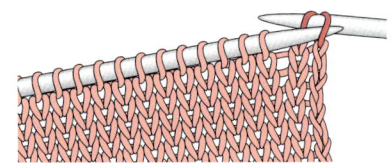

Pass first knitted stitch over the second stitch.

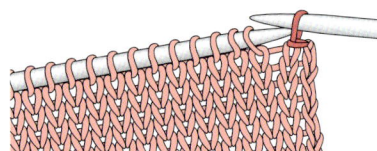

One bound-off knit stitch

2.  To bind off stitches on the wrong (or purl) side of your work, repeat step 1, but purl the stitches instead of knitting them.

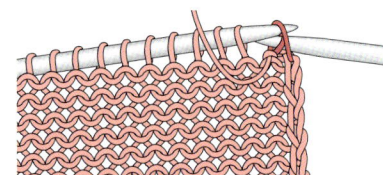

Pass first purled stitch over the second stitch.

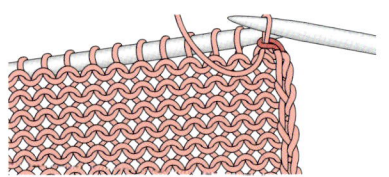

One bound-off purl stitch

## Backstitch Seams

I like to sew the side seams of a sweater and other vertical seams, such as the back seams of booties, by backstitching them. This process is similar to sewing two pieces of fabric together. Actually, if you like this technique, you can also use it to sew together an entire garment.

1.  Thread a tapestry needle with yarn that matches the knitting. Secure the beginning of the seam by bringing the yarn around the seam edges twice, and bring the needle back up approximately ¼" from where the yarn last emerged, as shown.

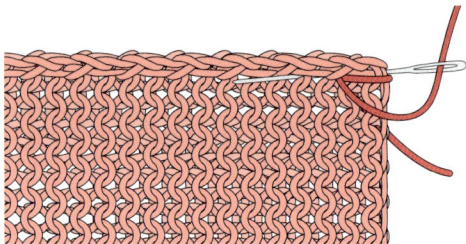

2.  In one motion, insert the needle into the point where the yarn emerged from the previous stitch and bring it back up approximately ¼" to the left. Pull the yarn through. Repeat, keeping your stitches even and loose so that the finished seam will be smooth, not puckered or distorted.

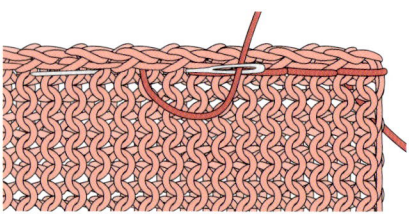

## Reading Charts

For patterns that feature color knitting in stockinette stitch, the patterns are presented on charts, which are much easier to read than written instructions. Each square of the chart equals one stitch, and each line of squares represents one row. The knit (or right-side, abbreviated RS) rows are odd-numbered rows and are read from right to left, in the same direction as you knit. The purl (or wrong-side, abbreviated WS) rows are even-numbered rows, and are read from left to right, in the same direction as you purl. The numbers for knit rows are shown at the right side of a chart, and the numbers for purl rows are shown at the left side. When you begin knitting, follow the rows of the chart from the bottom to the top, beginning with row 1. Each different color is represented by a different color on the chart. Sometimes it can be helpful to place a ruler just under the row you are working and move the ruler up as you work through the chart.

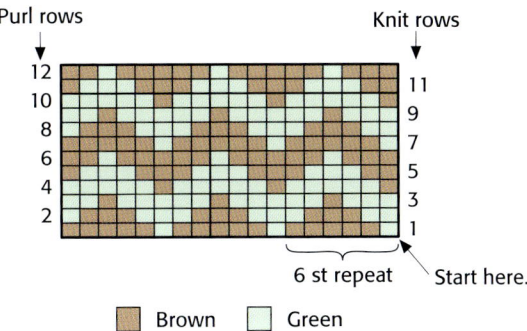

Brown ☐ Green

## Using Bobbins

When you need to knit with a few colors that are separated by wide expanses of a background color, bobbins are the perfect choice for holding the yarn in back of your work until you are ready to work with each color. Simply wind a small amount of each color of yarn around a bobbin and introduce each color wherever it is called for in the chart. When you begin working with a new color, take care to bring the bobbin color underneath the background color before you begin knitting with it; the yarns will twist together and prevent gaps between your stitches on the wrong side of your work. In the same manner, when you finish working with each color, bring the next color of yarn you want to work with underneath the bobbin yarn and begin knitting with the new color. Let the bobbin yarns hang at the back of your work when you are not working with them.

Bobbins for color-knitting

## Knitted Cords

Knitted cords make great additions to the tops of hats, and they are very easy to make. Simply cast on 3 or 4 stitches on a size 3 double-pointed needle. *Knit across, slide stitches back to the right end of the same needle, do not turn, and repeat from *. BO when you reach the desired length for the cord.

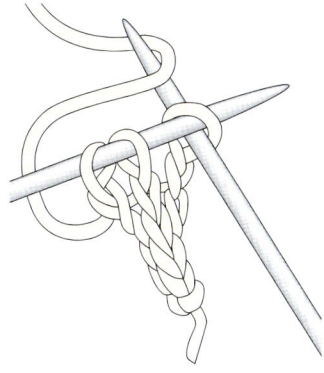

## Duplicate Stitching

Some of the garments in this book feature duplicate stitching, which looks just like knitted stitches when finished. Using these stitches to embellish a knitted garment is easy and fun.

1. To do horizontal duplicate stitching, thread a tapestry needle with the desired color of yarn. Bring the needle through from the wrong side of your work to the front side at the base of the knit stitch you wish to cover with a duplicate stitch. Then insert the needle under the base of the knitted stitch directly above the stitch you wish to cover.

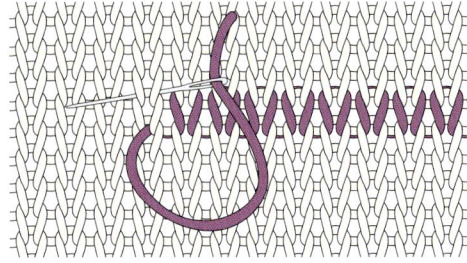

2. Bring the needle down and insert it at the base of the same knit stitch. Bring the tip of the needle out at the base of the next stitch you wish to cover, and repeat this process until you have covered all of the horizontal stitches

indicated in the project. When you reach the final duplicate stitch, pull the yarn all the way through to the wrong side and weave the end of the yarn through the back sides of your duplicate stitches.

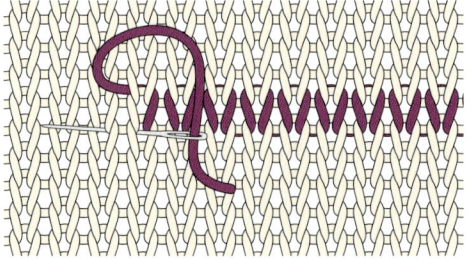

To do vertical duplicate stitching, bring a threaded tapestry needle through from the wrong side of your work to the front side, at the base of the first stitch to be covered. Insert the needle from right to left through the top of the same stitch. Bring the needle down and insert it at the base of the same stitch, bringing it out again at the base of the stitch that lies directly above the one you just covered. Continue in this manner until you reach the final vertical duplicate stitch; then pull the yarn all the way through to the wrong side and weave the tail end of the yarn through the back sides of your duplicate stitches.

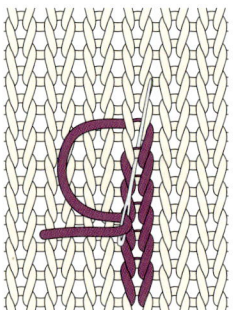

## French Knots

Thread a tapestry needle with the desired color of yarn, and bring the needle from the wrong to the right side of the knitted garment at the point where you wish to place a French knot. Holding the yarn down with your left thumb, wind the yarn twice around the needle (or more for larger knots). Still holding the yarn firmly, twist the needle back to the starting point and insert it close to where the yarn first emerged. Pull the yarn through to the wrong side of your knitting, creating a French knot on the surface of the garment. Take two or three whipstitches to secure the yarn on the wrong side of your work.

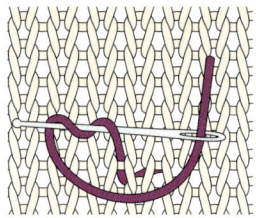

Wrap yarn around needle
2 or more times.

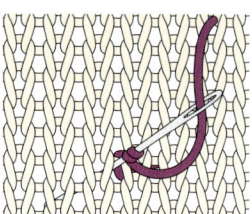

Insert yarn close to
emerging point.

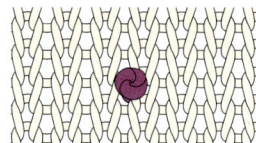

## Making Pompons

Pompons are a great way to top almost any style hat or bootie. You can make them as big or as little as you desire. Use one color of yarn, two for fun, or combine lots of colors for a confetti effect. You can buy pompon makers at craft stores. They usually come with three different-sized plastic disks that you can wrap yarn around until your pompon is as full as you want it to be. You can also cut a piece of heavy cardboard that has a height as wide as you want the diameter of your finished pompon to be. (A 3"-wide piece of cardboard will make a medium-sized pompon.) Wrap the yarn 40 or 50 times around the cardboard, or even more if you want to make a very full pompon. Cut an 18" strand of yarn, slip the wound loops off the cardboard, and use the strand of yarn to tie a very tight knot around the wound loops. Use a pair of scissors to cut through the loops of yarn on either side of the tied knot, and shake the pompon hard to fluff it out. Trim the ends evenly, if necessary.

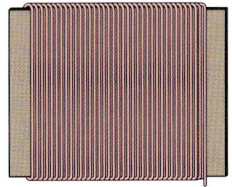

Wrap yarn 40 to 50 times around cardboard.

Tie a very tight knot around the yarn.

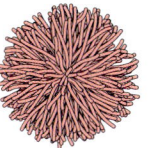

Clip loops. Trim evenly.

# Knitting Abbreviations

| | |
|---|---|
| approx | approximately |
| beg | begin(ning) |
| BO | bind off |
| ch | chain |
| circ | circular |
| CO | cast on |
| cont | continue |
| dc | double crochet |
| dec | decrease |
| dpn | double-pointed needle(s) |
| inc | increase |
| K | knit |
| K1f&b | knit in the front and in the back of the same stitch |
| K2tog | knit 2 stitches together |
| kw | knitwise |
| M1 | make 1 stitch |
| oz | ounce |
| P | purl |
| pat | pattern |
| psso | pass slipped stitch over |
| pw | purlwise |
| rem | remaining |
| rep | repeat |
| rnd | round |
| RS | right side |
| sc | single crochet |
| sl 1 | slip 1 stitch |
| st(s) | stitch(es) |
| St st | stockinette stitch |
| tog | together |
| WS | wrong side |
| wyib | with yarn in back |
| wyif | with yarn in front |
| yds | yards |
| yo | yarn over |

# Four-Point Berets

### Size: Newborn to 6 mos.

## Materials

- DK-weight cotton yarn in the following amounts and colors 🧶
  - ~ Approximately: 80 yds of desired main color
  - ~ Scraps of contrast colors for decorative elements
- 16" size 3 US circular needle
- 4 size 3 US double-pointed needles
- Stitch markers
- Tapestry needle

## Gauge

24 sts and 32 rows = 4" in St st

*I use the following pattern to make berets for toddlers and children of any age. (You can also use it to make a matching beret for yourself!) Choose the same colors I did, select your favorite colors, or use solid colors. There are no rules; whatever strikes your fancy is fine!*

## Bottom Band

Determine the number of stitches you will need to cast on by measuring around the head of the child for whom you are knitting. Multiply this number (inches) times 6 (the correct knitting gauge per inch). Adjust your number up or down a few stitches as needed to make sure that it is divisible by 4 (the crown of the beret has four sides). Cast on the number of sts you need on the circ needle. Place a st marker on the right needle and join your cast-on sts tog, making sure that the sts do not become twisted on the needle.

**Rnd 1:** Purl.

**Rnd 2:** Drop first color yarn (but do not cut). Attach a second color yarn and *K1, sl 1 wyib, K1*; rep from * to * until you reach st marker.

**Rnd 3:** With the same color as in last rnd, *P1, sl 1 wyib, P1*; rep from * to * to marker.

**Rnd 4:** Drop the second color, pick up first color, and K around.

**Rnd 5:** Purl.

> **TIP:** *You can vary the number of rows you work for the bottom band, add more colors, or even knit more than one bottom band, separating the bands by rnds of St st, which can be embellished creatively later.*

## Side Band and Points

With another color of your choice, K 11 rnds.

**Next rnd:** K, and divide your work into 4 equal sections, placing a st marker between each section.

**Inc rnd:** *K to 1 st before first st marker; K1f&b into that stitch; slip st marker onto right needle, K1, then K1f&b into second st from marker*; rep from * to * around.

Do 10 more inc rounds.

> **TIP:** *To make the side band higher, vary the number of knit rounds before you begin increasing.*

## Top Band

**Rnd 1:** With the same color as bottom band, knit.

**Rnd 2:** Purl.

**Rnd 3:** Drop first color yarn (but do not cut). Attach a new color yarn and *K1, sl 1 wyib, K1; rep from * to * around.

**Rnd 4:** With the same color as previous rnd, *P1, sl 1 wyib, P1*; rep from * to * around.

**Rnd 5:** Drop the second color and cut it. Pick up the first color; knit.

**Rnd 6:** Purl.

## Crown

**Dec rnd:** *K up to 2 sts before marker; K2tog, sl marker onto right needle, K1, K2tog*; rep from * to * around.

Cont working dec rnds in this manner, changing to 4 dpn when too few sts remain to cont using circ needle.

**Next rnd:** At this point, you can either BO all sts or finish with optional knitted cord (see below). For BO, when 8 sts remain, K2tog around, cut the yarn, and thread tail end through a tapestry needle to sew the sts tog, or finish the crown with a knitted cord.

## Finishing with a Knitted Cord

When 8 sts remain on dpn, keep working them using only 2 dpn, as follows: *K the sts, do not turn work. Instead, slide sts to right end of dpn, and pull yarn gently to tighten*. Rep from * to * to desired length. BO all sts, cut the yarn, thread the tail end through a tapestry needle, and push needle down through center of knitted cord for a neat finish. You can make the cord 1" to 2" long and add a button or bead at the end, or make the cord long enough that you can tie a knot at the top of the beret.

> **TIP:** *To produce interesting concentric squares, use contrasting colors to work a pattern of stripes in the crown of the beret.*

## Creative Embellishments

Decorating children's berets is a lot of fun. Try some of these ideas, and enjoy coming up with some more of your own!

**Note:** Consider the age of the child carefully when deciding whether or not to embellish a beret with buttons and beads, which present a choking hazard to small children.

## Bobbles

With RS facing and main color, work to where you want the first bobble, drop main color yarn. With new color yarn, K1, P1, K1 in next st (making 3 sts from 1). Turn and K3. Turn and K3, lift second and third sts over first st. Drop the bobble yarn and pick up main color again. Work to next place for bobble, carrying the bobble yarn along the WS of work if the next bobble is 5 sts or less from the first bobble. Be sure to carry yarns loosely on WS to avoid distorting the knitting. If the bobbles will be more than 5 sts apart, cut the yarn after each bobble leaving a tail long enough to weave in, and start with a new strand of yarn for the next bobble.

## Spirals

CO 15 sts.

**Row 1:** (K1f&b, K1) in each st.

**Row 2:** BO all sts pw. Rep to make as many spirals as desired; attach to top of crown.

## Pompons

You can decorate berets with a single pompon at each point or with a cascade of them. Refer to "Making Pompons" on page 9 for instructions.

## French Knots

Refer to page 8 for instructions on making French knots. Use them on the side bands and crown, wherever you like.

## Duplicate-Stitch Motifs

The following designs are great for decorating the side bands of a beret. Add them after you finish making the beret, referring to "Duplicate Stitching" on page 7. The number of sts in each rep is given on each chart; space the designs as needed to fit the number of sts in the side band of your beret. You can place the designs side by side or vary the number of sts between each motif.

**Chick pattern**

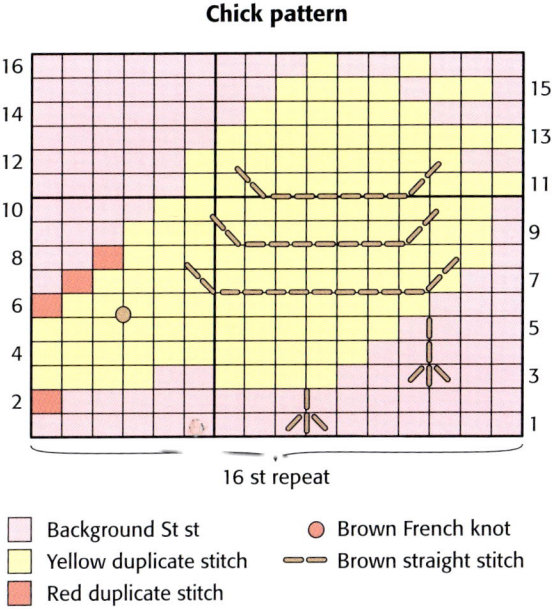

16 st repeat

◻ Background St st     ● Brown French knot

◻ Yellow duplicate stitch     ⚊⚊ Brown straight stitch

◻ Red duplicate stitch

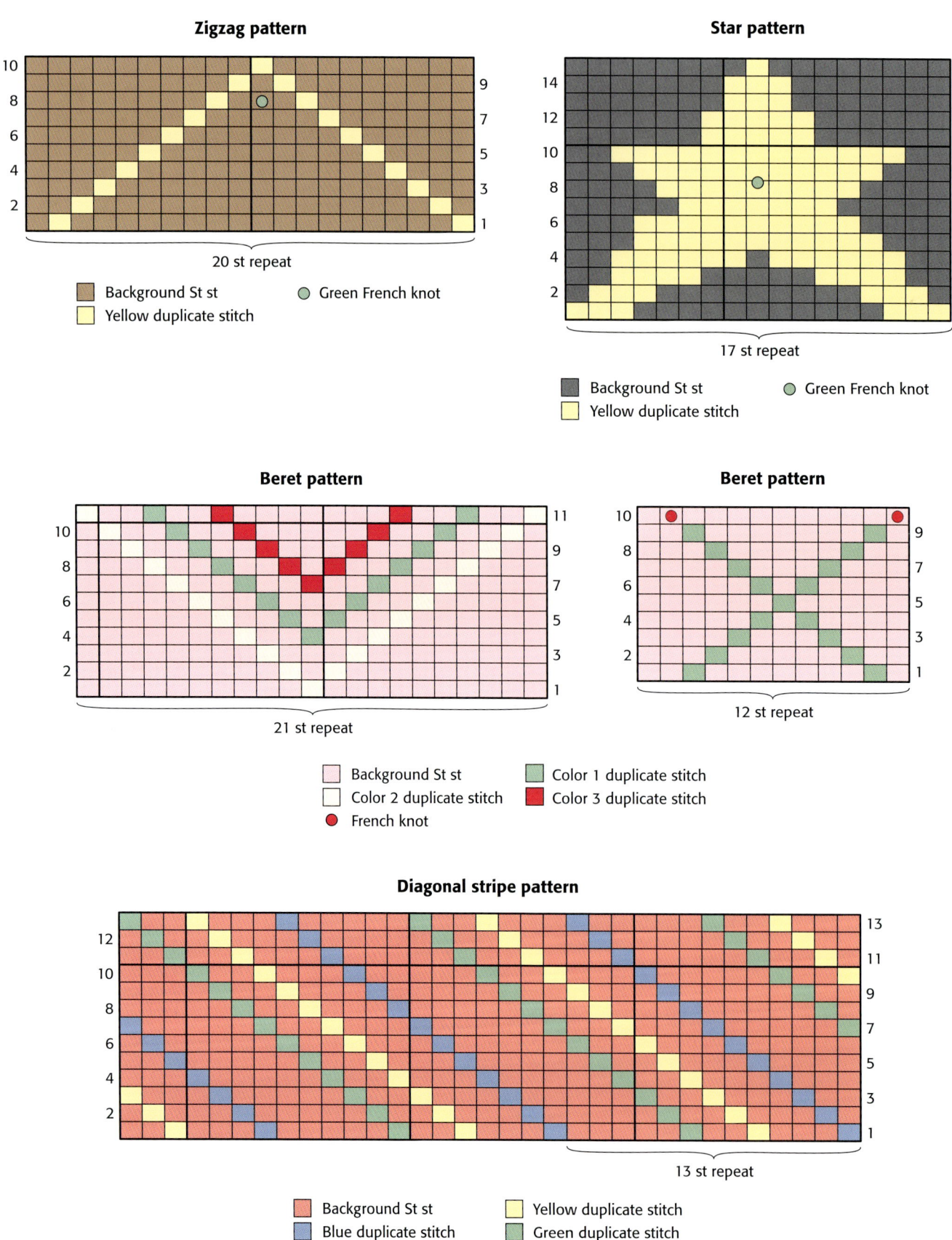

### Zigzag pattern

20 st repeat

■ Background St st    ● Green French knot
□ Yellow duplicate stitch

### Star pattern

17 st repeat

■ Background St st    ● Green French knot
□ Yellow duplicate stitch

### Beret pattern

21 st repeat

### Beret pattern

12 st repeat

□ Background St st    ■ Color 1 duplicate stitch
□ Color 2 duplicate stitch    ■ Color 3 duplicate stitch
● French knot

### Diagonal stripe pattern

13 st repeat

■ Background St st    □ Yellow duplicate stitch
■ Blue duplicate stitch    ■ Green duplicate stitch

# Bobble Beanie

**Size: Newborn to 6 mos.**

## Materials

- DK-weight cotton yarn in the following amounts and colors: 🔳3🔳
  ~ Approximately 40 yds each of red, yellow, pink, blue, black, and green
- 16" size 3 US circular needle
- 4 size 3 US double-pointed needles
- Stitch markers
- Tapestry needle

## Gauge

24 sts and 32 rows = 4" in St st

*These playful little hats are a great place to use small amounts of leftover yarns in creative color combinations. Making them is a lot like eating potato chips—it's hard to stop at one!*

## Pattern Stitch—Bobbles

With RS facing in main color, work to place for first bobble, drop main color yarn. With new color yarn, K1, P1, K1 in next st (making 3 sts from 1). Turn and K3. Turn and K3, lift second and third sts over first st. Drop the bobble yarn and pick up main color again. Work to next place for bobble, carrying the bobble yarn along the WS of work. Be sure to carry yarns loosely on WS to avoid distorting the knitting.

## Red-and-Yellow Bottom Band

With circ needle and yellow, CO 102 sts. Place a st marker on right needle and join CO sts tog, making sure that sts do not become twisted on needle.

**Rnd 1:** Purl.

**Rnd 2:** Drop yellow yarn (but do not cut). Attach red yarn and *K1, sl 1 wyib*; rep from * to * around.

**Rnd 3:** *P1, sl 1 wyib*; rep from * to * around.

**Rnd 4:** With yellow, knit.

**Rnd 5:** Purl.

## Red-and-Yellow Bobble Band

**Rnds 1 and 2:** With red, knit.

**Rnd 3:** *With yellow, make bobble in next st; with red, K5*; rep from * to * around.

**Rnds 4 and 5:** With red, knit.

## Red-and-Yellow Band

Rep 5 rnds of red-and-yellow bottom band.

## Green-and-Blue Band

**Rnd 1:** With green, purl.

**Rnd 2:** Drop green yarn (but do not cut). Attach blue yarn and *K1, sl 1 wyib*; rep from * to * around.

**Rnd 3:** *P1, sl 1 wyib*; rep from * to * around.

**Rnd 4:** With green, knit.

**Rnd 5:** Purl.

## Green-and-Blue Bobble Band

**Rnds 1 and 2:** With blue, knit.

**Rnd 3:** *With green, make bobble in next st; with blue, K5*; rep from * to * around.

**Rnds 4 and 5:** With blue, knit.

## Green-and-Blue Band

Rep 5 rnds of green-and-blue band.

## Pink-and-Yellow Band

**Rnd 1:** With pink, purl.

**Rnd 2:** Drop pink yarn (but do not cut). Attach yellow yarn and *K1, sl 1 wyib*; rep from * to * around.

**Rnd 3:** *P1, sl 1 wyib*; rep from * to * around.

**Rnd 4:** With pink, purl.

**Rnd 5:** Knit.

## Pink-and-Yellow Bobble Band

**Rnds 1 and 2:** With yellow, knit.

**Rnd 3:** *With pink, make bobble in next st, with yellow, K5*; rep from * to * around.

**Rnds 4 and 5:** With yellow, knit.

## Pink-and-Yellow Band

Rep 5 rnds of pink-and-yellow band.

## Black Top Band

**Rnd 1:** With black, knit.

**Rnd 2:** *K6, K2tog*; rep from * to * around.

**Rnd 3:** *K5, K2tog*; rep from * to * around.

**Rnd 4:** *K4, K2tog*; rep from * to * around.

**Rnd 5:** *K3, K2tog*; rep from * to * around.

**Rnd 6:** *K2, K2tog*; rep from * to * around. Cont in this pat, changing to dpn when necessary. When 4 sts rem, BO all sts.

## Adding the Spirals

Referring to "Spirals" on page 13, make 5 spirals, one each in green, pink, blue, red, and yellow. Sew them to the top of the beanie.

# Christmas Tree Hats

*These little yuletide "tree toppers" are so fast and easy to make, you may want to whip up several to give as Christmas gifts to small family members and their friends.*

## Size: Newborn to 6 mos.

## Materials

- DK-weight cotton yarn in the following amounts and colors: **3**
  - ~ Approximately:
  - ~ 100 yds bright green or forest green
  - ~ 40 yds red
  - ~ 40 yds yellow
  - ~ 40 yds teal

- 16" size 3 US circular needle

- 4 size 3 US double-pointed needles

- Stitch markers

- Tapestry needle

## Gauge
24 sts and 32 rows = 4" in St st

## Hat Base

With circ needle and green, CO 100 sts. Place a st marker on right needle and join CO sts tog, making sure that sts do not become twisted on needle.

**Rnd 1:** K, placing a st marker at halfway point of rnd.

**Rnds 2–8:** Knit.

**Dec rnd:** K to 2 sts from first marker, K2tog, K to 2 sts from second marker, K2tog.

Cont knitting each rnd, working a dec rnd on every other rnd. When 50 sts remain, beg working every rnd as a dec rnd, switching to dpn when necessary.

When 26 sts rem, K2tog around entire rnd. Rep until approx 6 sts remain. BO all sts. Cut the yarn, thread the tail end through a tapestry needle, and weave the yarn through several sts on WS of work.

## Garlands

With yellow, and referring to "Knitted Cords" on page 7, make a knitted cord that is long enough to wind around the hat several times, beg at the bottom edge and spiraling up to tip of hat. On WS, tack knitted garland in place with matching yarn.

> **TIP:** *Just for fun, as you knit the rounds of the hat, you can knit 1 round in a contrasting color every so many rounds to form a knitted-in garland.*

## Pompons and Spirals

Embellish tip of tree hat with colorful pompons, referring to "Making Pompons" on page 9, or add some knitted spirals, referring to "Spirals" on page 13.

## French Knots

With red, and referring to "French Knots" on page 8, add French knots to the hat, spacing them randomly between the garlands.

> **TIP:** *To make a Christmas Tree Hat in a different size, use a tape measure to measure around the head of the child you are knitting for. Multiply this number (inches) times 6 (the correct knitting gauge per inch). Cast on this number of sts (rounding up to an even number if your measurement yields an odd number) and follow the directions as given on these pages.*

# Booties

These booties are quite small, and made for babies to wear before they start to walk. Because baby booties tend to get themselves lost very easily, I like to make three booties in each style. They are quick and easy to make and lots of fun to decorate. Use the following basic bootie instructions for all of the booties shown in the photos and see if you can think up some more creative ways to embellish them.

## Size: Newborn (3–6 mos.)

## Materials

- DK-weight cotton yarn in the following amounts and colors: **3**
  ~ Small amounts of leftover yarn totaling approximately 60 yards for each bootie
- 1 pair size 3 US straight needles
- Stitch markers
- Stitch holders
- Tapestry needle

## Gauge

24 sts and 32 rows = 4" in St st

*Note:* The following instructions are for the smaller size. The numbers for the larger size are given in parentheses. Where only 1 number is given, it applies to both sizes.

## Pattern Stitch

### Garter Stitch

Knit all rows.

## Top

CO 26 (34) sts for top portion of bootie.

Work 5 rows in garter st. Insert a st marker on the last row, to mark it as WS of bootie.

**Beading row (RS):** *K2, yo, K2tog*; rep from * to *, ending K2.

Work 5 (11) more rows (or as many rows as necessary to make the top part as long as desired) in garter st and cut yarn.

## Instep

Place the first 9 (12) sts on a st holder. Rejoin same color yarn as for bootie top, K across next 8 (10) sts for instep, place the last 9 (12) sts on a st holder, turn work.

Working on 8 (10) instep sts only, work 9 (11) rows in garter st, ending on WS row. Cut yarn.

Place first 9 (12) sts from st holder onto needle.

**Row 1 (RS):** Join new yarn, K9 (12) sts, pick up 9 (12) sts along side edge of instep, knit across 8 (10) instep sts, pick up 9 (12) sts along other side edge of instep, K9 (12) sts from second st holder—44 (58) sts.

Work 16 rows in garter st, ending with WS facing for next row.

## Welt

With WS facing, *sl the first st from the left to the right needle; count down 3 ridges on the WS of garter st rows, pick up and knit the top loop of the first st on this ridge, pass the first st over the new st*; rep from * to *—44 (58) sts.

Knit 1 row.

## Sole

**Row 1:** With the same color, or a new color of your choice, K1, K2tog, K19 (26) sts, place st marker on needle; K to last 3 sts, K2tog, K1.

**Row 2:** Knit to 2 sts from st marker, K2tog, K1, K2tog, K to end.

Rep last row 4 times. BO all sts.

Rep from "Top" to make second (and third) bootie.

## Finishing

Sew the seams of booties, referring to "Backstitch Seams" on page 6.

## Knitted Cords

Referring to "Knitted Cords" on page 7, CO 4 sts and make 1 knitted cord approximately 24" long for each bootie. Thread cord through beading row on each bootie and tie cord in a bow.

*This pair of booties has corded strings and pompons to keep an active baby entertained.*

*It takes only small amounts of brightly colored yarn to create these adorable booties.*

## Sweet Booties

Follow the bootie instructions on page 20 to make small or large booties. Substitute seed st for garter st on the top part of each bootie and use pink for instep and welt and green for soles. With green, make 1 knitted cord for each bootie, referring to "Knitted Cords" on page 7.

## Flower Booties

Follow the bootie instructions on page 20 to make small or large booties in the colors of your choice.

## Flowers

*(Refer to instructions below as needed.)*

To crochet a small flower: Make a chain of 6 sts; join into a circle. *Ch 3, 3dc into the circle, ch 3 and sc into the circle; rep from * 4 more times, sc into the circle. Cut yarn, thread the tail end through a tapestry needle, and weave it through a few sts on wrong side of the flower. Make a flower for each bootie and attach with a French knot to top of bootie.

*Make these fun pink booties for a special little girl you know.*

## Chain Stitch

1. Make a slip knot in the yarn. Wrap the yarn over the hook and draw the yarn through the loop to form a new loop.

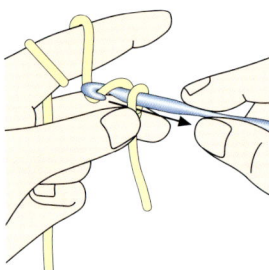

2. Repeat to form as many chains as required.

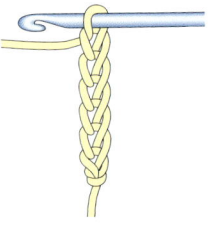

## Double Crochet

1. Wrap yarn around hook and insert the hook into the stitch.

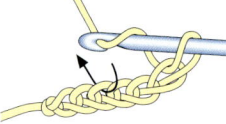

2. Wrap yarn around hook and pull yarn through the stitch to the front of the work

3. Wrap yarn around hook and pull yarn through 2 loops on the hook.

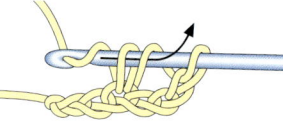

4. Wrap yarn around hook and pull yarn through 2 remaining loops on the hook.

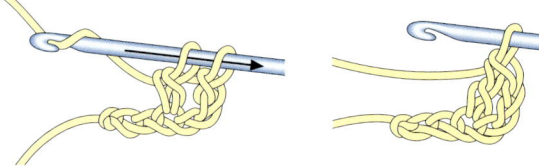

*The classic Mary Jane shoe takes on a playful air when made in miniature.*

*Who could resist these creative little critters? Make them in a rainbow of colors to delight your favorite little ones.*

## Mary Janes

Follow the bootie instructions on page 20 to make small or large booties.

**To make strap:** CO 3 sts. Work 10 rows in garter st. BO all sts. Rep to make a second strap. Sew straps to booties and add a button at one end of each strap.

## Animal Booties

Follow the bootie instructions on page 20 to make small or large booties. Add French knots (see page 8) to front of each bootie for a nose and eyes. Embroider a smile. If desired, make whiskers with scrap yarn. You can also make a very short spiral for a tail on each bootie.

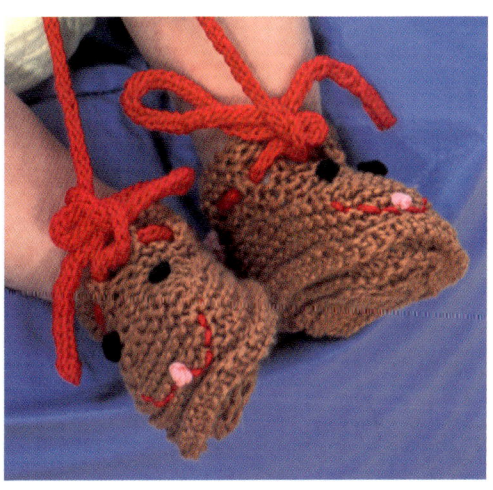

*Here's a closer look at these cute booties!*

# About the Author

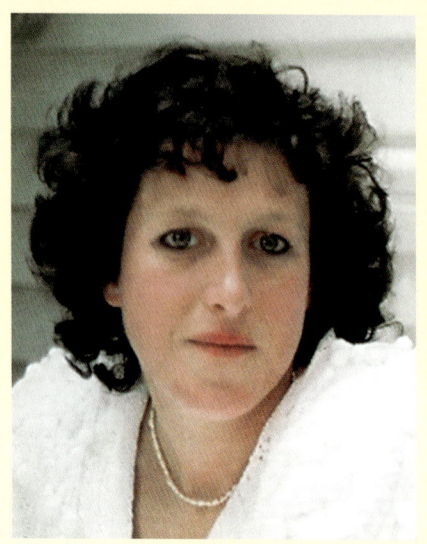

**Debby Ware** discovered knitting as a child when her mother taught her the basics, and she has loved it ever since. After graduating from the School of Visual Arts in New York City, she worked for various freelance designers knitting swatches, and also loved to make one-of-a-kind sweaters for her family and friends. Eventually Debby moved from the city to Martha's Vineyard, where she owned two businesses with each of her sisters and where she sold her knitted creations. She eventually started a small business of her own, Debby Ware Knitwares, through which she continues to design and produce her wonderful knitting patterns and kits for babies and toddlers. She has given up the ocean for the mountains and now lives on a hilltop in Rapidan, Virginia, with her husband, Will, son Owen, Bessie Basset Hound, Buster the Cat, and Lucky the Dog. Find more of Debby's patterns at www.debbyware.com.